Addicted to His Presence

BETH STEWART

Foreword by Mike Kalfas, MD, FAAFP

Endorsements for
Addicted to His Presence

"*Addicted to His Presence* is a great start for true recovery of addictions."
Mike Kalfas, MD, FAAFP, certified addiction specialist by the American Board of Addiction Medicine and member of the Northern Kentucky Heroin Impact

"I've learned that prayer—getting into His presence—is to our spirit man what air is to our natural man. It's the key to living a victorious life, free of addiction. In *Addicted to His Presence*, Beth Stewart not only unlocks this truth, but also shares how you can experience His presence for yourself. Whether you're struggling daily to overcome an addiction or not, this book is for you."
Lawrence Bishop II, co-pastor of Solid Rock Church; founder of Hope Over Heroin

"Working on the front lines of the war on addiction, I have witnessed the devastation from people using worldly pleasures to fill voids in their lives. This book provides hope and freedom from addiction through a personal relationship with God who offers true fulfillment."
Debora Reeves LCSW, LCADC, co-owner and therapist/alcohol & drug treatment supervisor of Land of Goshen Treatment Center & Lighthouse Professional Counseling Services

"*ADDICTION* is not a bad word. Beth Stewart's new book does an incredible job of bringing to light the benefits of being *addicted* to the presence of GOD. Good read!"
Carl Behanan, station manager, Christian Broadcasting System

"*Addicted to His Presence* is a real eye opener, full of insight, revelation, and knowledge. A must read for every person who is struggling with hurts, hang-ups, or habits."
James Turner, founder and president of Bridge the Gap Ministries and US Urban Missionary

"Freedom to walk in your God-given destiny is possible when you partner with your Creator and embrace the biblical principles outlined in this life-changing book."
Terri Meredith, Terri Meredith Ministries

"We all were created to worship God and being in His Presence always brings life-changing transformation. *Addicted to His Presence* paints the picture of what it is like to experience God's Presence. This book is a first step to your own personal transformation with the living God."
Sheila Salisbury-Sizemore, instructor, Christian Healing Certification Program, Global Awakening

"Simple and easy to understand, yet incredibly powerful!"
Jennifer Minigh, Ph.D., Owner, ShadeTree Publishing

BethStewartMinistries.com

Do you try to fill an emptiness in your being with activities, substances, or unhealthy relationships? If so, then this book is for you. Unlike other books that focus on the physical side of addiction, *Addicted to His Presence* addresses the spiritual side of addiction and gets to the root cause of the problem. The bottom line is that the only healthy addiction is being addicted to God's presence, and this book shows you how to find it and keep it.

ADDICTED TO HIS PRESENCE
Beth Stewart
Foreword by Mina "Mike" Kalfas, MD, FAAFP
Copyright @ 2015 Beth Stewart Ministries
Print ISBN: 978-0-9909447-2-0
e-Book ISBN: 978-0-9909447-3-7

Scripture quotations marked NIV are taken from the HOLY BIBLE, NEW INTERNATIONAL VERSION®. Copyright © 1973, 1978, 1984 International Bible Society. Used by permission of Zondervan. All rights reserved.

Scripture quotations marked NKJV are taken from the New King James Version®. Copyright © 1982 by Thomas Nelson, Inc. All rights reserved.

Scripture quotations marked KJV are taken from the King James Version. The KJV is public domain in the United States.

All rights reserved. This book is protected by copyright. No part of this book may be reproduced or transmitted in any form or by any means, electronic or mechanical, including photocopying, recording, or by any information storage and retrieval system, without permission in writing from the publisher.

The purpose of this book is to educate and enlighten. This book is sold with the understanding that the author and publisher are not engaged in rendering counseling, albeit it professional or lay, to the reader or anyone else. The author and publisher shall have neither liability nor responsibility to any person or entity with respect to any loss or damage caused, or alleged to have been caused, directly or indirectly, by the information contained in this book.

Visit our Web site at BethStewartMinistries.com.

I dedicate the book to my sister Karen Sue Sallie, who struggled with many addiction issues but who gave her life to Christ toward the end. Even though her life ended far too soon, I am comforted in knowing that she accepted Christ and that the grace of God escorted her into her heavenly home.

CONTENTS

Foreword by Mina "Mike" Kalfas, MD, FAAFP 1
Preface 5
Chapter 1 WHAT IS "HIS PRESENCE"? 9
Chapter 2 WHAT ARE ADDICTIONS? 19
Chapter 3 BECOMING ADDICTED TO HIS PRESENCE 35
Chapter 4 BENEFITS OF BEING ADDICTED TO HIS PRESENCE . 47
Chapter 5 EVIDENCE OF BEING ADDICTED TO HIS PRESENCE 59
Chapter 6 REMAINING IN HIS PRESENCE 69
Chapter 7 YOU CAN AND YOU WILL OVERCOME 83
About the Author 87
About Beth Stewart Ministries 91
Acknowledgments 93
Review Request 95
Scriptures and Reference 97

Beth Stewart

FOREWORD BY
Mina "Mike" Kalfas, MD, FAAFP

As a young family physician exiting my residency program and starting practice in a rural community, I thought that my modern training at the University of Kentucky College of medicine and residency training in Cincinnati at Bethesda Family Practice had prepared me for anything. However, there were two things that the Lord had in store for me, yet: a much deeper walk with Him and caring for those with addictions.

Despite being raised in a Christian home and having a Christian marriage, I still had a lot of spiritual growth ahead of me. Specifically, I had a lot of "me" to be purged of and a lot of the Spirit to be filled with. Likewise, nothing in my medical training would prepare me for the heroin epidemic that would explode onto the scene in my native Northern Kentucky area. I found myself being led on both spiritual and professional journeys simultaneously. Journeys of awakening and learning. Looking back, I see God's hand in it so clearly.

As a physician, I had been trained to look at disease—the dysfunction, the breakdown, the sickness, and the failure in an organ or system, if you will, that leads to it. When it comes to addiction, though, many physicians initially blow off a patient as one who lacks the willpower or determination to stop. These providers believe that spirituality of some sort is necessary to overcome the disease of addiction (if they are even willing to *call* it a disease).

When I finally acknowledged that addiction is a disease, I was at a personal point in my life where I was keenly aware of the concept of spiritual warfare. I recognized the dual nature of addiction as both a physical disease and a spiritual battle. As such, the "cure" is one that must be approached from a dualistic standpoint or it will be incomplete. We must not treat the body and neglect the spirit.

My observations and experiences have taught me that a transforming, lasting, and life-changing recovery from addiction is one in which God is central. God created us so that He could dwell within us as the Holy Spirit. Our bodies are therefore a temple of the Holy Spirit. Too often, we pollute our bodies and thereby desecrate the place where the Holy Spirit is supposed to dwell, leaving a void in our lives. It can thus be said that the essence of addiction is a deficiency of the Holy Spirit with a poor substitute in its place. The only true treatment of addiction is the correction of this deficiency. This book, *Addicted to His Presence*, is a great start for true recovery of addictions.

About Dr. Mike Kalfas

Dr. Kalfas is a family medicine practitioner who received his medical degree at the University of Kentucky College of Medicine and completed his residency at the Bethesda Family Practice Program in Cincinnati. He is certified by the American Board of Family Practice, is a fellow of the Fellow American Board of Family Practice, and is a certified addiction specialist by the American Board of Addiction Medicine.

He joined The Christ Hospital Physicians after practicing for fifteen years as a primary care physician. He is also the former medical director of the St. Elizabeth Alcohol and Drug Treatment Center. He serves currently on the Northern Kentucky Heroin Impact Response Team.

Dr. Kalfas regularly attends church, where he teaches and serves on the praise team and various other ministry teams.

Preface

Are you hungry for more than what your life is now? Do you try to fill an emptiness in your being with activities, substances, or unhealthy relationships? If so, then I have good news for you. First of all, you're not alone, and second, there is a cure and I have experienced it in my own life. The only thing that can fill the void inside of you and bring you peace and satisfaction is the presence of the Lord.

The presence of God is not a theology. It is the real manifestation of God Almighty—Himself—to bring transformation into your life. Once you experience God's presence, even for a brief moment, it will change you forever. You will go from *knowing about God* to *knowing God intimately*. God is alive and real, but until you experience Him for yourself, it may be hard to understand that concept.

I was raised in a very conservative denominational church, and throughout my childhood and early teens, I never really felt God's presence. Don't get me wrong—I knew God was always there and that He loved me, because the songs we sang in Vacation Bible School and Sunday school said so.

It wasn't until I was seventeen years old that I first witnessed the presence of God. My mother had just received the Holy Spirit, and she asked me to go to a Spirit-filled revival with her. We sat in the auditorium full of people who were outwardly expressing their love for God during worship. They were raising their hands and shouting "amen," which was something I was definitely not used to in our conservative church. I would glance at my mom from time to time and notice tears flowing down her cheeks. This was something new to me, as well, because my mother was not one to show much emotion, especially in church. Something different was happening to her. That night, I witnessed her experiencing the presence of God.

After seeing God move upon my mother's heart, I began looking for Him in everyday life. One time my mom was perplexed by a strange odor in the house. Despite her repeated searches, she could not find the origin of the stench. My mother, who was just learning about the realities of a living God herself and beginning to exercise her childlike faith, decided to pray and ask Him to show her the source of the smell. (I personally thought this was ludicrous, believing that God surely had bigger and better things to do than search for the source of a smell.) Immediately after her prayer, we heard a noisy commotion coming from the kitchen and quickly discovered that the curtains had mysteriously fallen from the window. When my mother started to return them to their rightful place, she noticed a small rotten tomato sitting in a corner of the windowsill that had been previously hidden by the hanging curtains. I know it may sound silly to many of you, but that little rotten tomato was monumental to my faith. It revealed a God who cares about every tiny detail in our lives. He became alive and very personal to me.

I continued to encounter signs and wonders in my personal life and started sensing God working around me. My eyes became opened, and my spirit was awakened to a new reality—that God's presence is real, even in my own life. Throughout my adult life, it has been the presence of God that has sustained me, not religion.

Encountering God's presence was the greatest life-changing experience I have ever had. Not too long ago, the Lord spoke to my heart and softly spoke a scripture to me: "Freely you have received, freely give."[1] I knew that He was nudging me to share with others all the truths that would set people free, including myself. It is my prayer that this book leads you and others to find the place and power of God's presence in your lives.

Chapter 1
WHAT IS "HIS PRESENCE"?

To completely understand what "His presence" is, we first need to travel back in time…

His Presence in the Beginning

In the beginning, when God created Adam and Eve, He placed them in the Garden of Eden, where they enjoyed His undefiled presence continuously. Every day in this paradise, they personally fellowshipped with the Lord and experienced perfect peace and health. Completely foreign to them were confusion, depression, mental torment, illness, shame, loneliness, grief, or death.

Separation from His Presence

Also in the Garden during this time, however, was the one who fell from heaven because he sought to be worshiped above the Lord. As an angel in heaven, his name had been

Lucifer, but as the demon leader on earth, he became known as Satan, the serpent, the evil one, and the father of all lies. This cursed one wriggled into the lives of Adam and Eve and sowed doubt and deception into their minds concerning God's command about eating the fruit from the Tree of the Knowledge of Good and Evil. They partook of the fruit, and as a result of their disobedience, sin entered the world and death was born.

Now mankind was forever steeped in sin and thus were separated from the holiness of God. Adam and Eve were forced to leave the Garden, no longer able to dwell in the presence of God. From this point on, man could only approach God through the priests in the Temple. Forever lost was the ability to personally experience the undefiled presence of God.

GETTING BACK TO HIS PRESENCE

Human beings were created with an innate desire to bask continually in God's presence. Since the fall of man into sin and the consequential separation from God, humans have been left with a void in their lives, giving rise to a desperate longing to fill it. God allows this yearning in our beings so that we will seek Him. He longs for us as much as we long for Him. Herein lies the quest of our spirits to return to the undefiled presence of God.

Jesus Is the Door

It is our destiny to return to the presence of God, but because we are now steeped in the original sin of Adam and Eve, we must understand that we are all sinners and need a Savior. Jesus is the remedy to our dilemma.

Our heavenly Father used Jesus to provide a way for all of us to return to Him.

> *Jesus answered, "I am the way and the truth and the life. No one comes to the Father except through me."*
> —John 14:6 NIV

The Bible says that "the wages of sin is death."[2] In other words, if someone dies with sin in his or her life, then he or she will experience eternal death. When Jesus was crucified on the cross, all of our sin was laid upon Him. He died with our sins so that we wouldn't have to. Because He took our sin, we were made righteous and can now enter into the presence of God.

Jesus is the Door to God's presence. There is no other way to return to the presence of God than accepting Jesus as our Savior. We must first walk through this Door before we can begin our journey back to the Father.

> *Then said Jesus unto them again, Verily, verily, I say unto you, I am the door of the sheep.*
> —John 10:7 KJV

Seek Him and You Will Find Him

Once we have accepted Jesus as our Savior and have walked through that Door, we are on our way to finding the presence of the Lord. Our next step is to seek Him.

> *"You will seek me and find me when you seek me with all your heart."*
> —Jeremiah 29:13 NIV

What does it mean "to seek"? Seeking is an action that requires effort; it does not happen passively. Imagine a mother who is accidentally separated from her young son in a shopping mall. Does the mother continue to shop while casually looking around every now and then for her child? Of course not! The mother drops everything and begins an active and intentional search for the child. So should our search be for God—full of intent and desperation to find Him.

The last part of Jeremiah 29:13 contains the phrase "with all your heart" (NIV). Just like with the mother searching for her son, our search for God's presence must be committed and focused. That mother is not mentally making a shopping list or contemplating a new recipe while she is looking for her child. No! *All of her heart* is set on finding her child, just like *all of our heart* should be set on finding Him.

People tell me all the time that they seek God but cannot find Him, but I would beg to differ. The problem is not that they cannot find Him; rather, they are likely having trouble perceiving Him. If God said that He would be there, then you can be sure He will be, regardless of whether you feel Him or not. Many times, God shows up in ways we are not expecting, so our radar may be off in that area. Sometimes He is in the creation all around us, or He may speak to us on the wind. If you are having trouble sensing the Lord's presence today, just ask Him for help. Tell Him that you don't detect Him and ask Him to reveal Himself more clearly as you turn up your sensors. This request is just another way of actively seeking Him and believing with faith that He is really there (which He loves).

How to Approach the Presence of God

With Clean Hands and a Pure Heart
The Word of God says that we need to have clean hands and a pure heart to enter the presence of God.

> *Who may stand in his holy place? He who has clean hands and a pure heart.*
> —Psalm 24:3–4 NIV

Revelation 7:14 says that the blood of Jesus has washed us clean from sin. Even though our spirits are washed clean, though, sometimes our earthly hands and body can dabble in sin and get dirty. We can still get blood on our hands, so to speak, and when our hands are dirty, our conscience is, too.

Addicted to His Presence

In Shakespeare's famous play, *Macbeth*, Lady Macbeth compulsively washed her hands in an attempt to remove the blood that symbolized her guilt.[3] In Matthew 27:24, Pilate "washed his hands in front of the crowd" as a symbolic act, and he declared his innocence in condemning Jesus to death. As for us, before we enter the presence of God, we need to wash our hands—and our hearts.

When I start out seeking the Lord's presence, I ask God to search my heart and my ways, to reveal any wickedness or sin within me.[4] If He exposes anything, I immediately seek His forgiveness and repent of my actions, motives, or thoughts. When God sheds light on my problem areas, I also push back the temptation to get offended, which is sometimes a natural reaction when we come under inspection. Jesus said, "Blessed is he who is not offended because of Me."[5] Proverbs 19:11 says that a person's wisdom will yield patience, and it brings a person glory when he or she overlooks an offense. In other words, a wise person has patience and is not easily offended.

A heart that takes offense is not a heart of repentance. Repentance is a concept greatly misunderstood in our world today. Many people think it just means to say we are sorry and apologize for our actions; however, it actually means something far more potent. By definition, to *repent* means "to turn from sin and dedicate oneself to the amendment of one's life."[6] Repentance requires us to change our point of view to match up with God's. Basically, we must stop in our tracks, make a 180-degree turn, and go in the opposite direction. This is very different from simply saying we are sorry, but then continuing to do bad things.

Many people have told me they have repented of certain sins, but yet there is no evidence of their claims because they continue in their wrongdoings. One such story involves a young man who was bound by alcohol and drug addictions. About once every six months, he would go to church, pray at the altar, and be baptized; however, he continued in his bad habits and did not seek help in escaping them. He never truly repented, and he was never fully able to enter the presence of God.

Like a lack of repentance, unforgiveness toward ourselves and others will soil our hearts and keep us away from the presence of God. The Bible cautions against unforgiveness and urges us not to let any root of bitterness spring up in our hearts and defile us.[7] It also says that when we are seeking the Lord, if we remember someone who has something against us, we are to stop what we are doing and go make amends with that person, before entering God's presence.[8] We must have clean hands and a pure heart when we approach the Lord.

By Grace

The reason we need to discuss grace at this point is because without an understanding of it, you may never fully believe you are worthy to approach the Lord, and thereby you may never experience His presence in the fullness of what He intends for you to experience.

So, what is grace? Grace is the free and unmerited favor of God. It cannot be earned because it is freely given to us.[9] We gain access to grace by having faith in Jesus,[10] and we are saved and justified by it.[11] Our works and good deeds, regardless of how noble and altruistic they may be, can never make us worthy enough to approach the Lord—but the Lord says that His grace is sufficient for us.[12]

People who have trouble accepting God's grace in their lives may be struggling with issues of shame or unworthiness. Years ago, I ministered to a young girl who needed a touch of God so desperately in her life. I was trying to help her understand how to approach God, but she would tell me that she was too afraid. When I would ask her about her fears, her answer was always the same: She would list all the things she had done wrong in her life. She had fallen into the enemy's trap of condemnation, and she felt unworthy to approach a holy God. I explained to her that we all have sinned and fallen short of God's glory, but grace is the Father's overwhelming desire to treat us as if we had never sinned.

Don't let condemnation or thoughts of your own unworthiness prevent you from approaching God. Remember that we all deal with these negative emotions—but we must come to the understanding that we can approach Him because we have been given the grace to do so. Because the blood of Jesus covers all our sin, His blood is what God sees first when we approach Him.

With Boldness
The Word of God is very clear about how we should approach His throne.

> *Let us therefore come boldly unto the throne...*
> —Hebrews 4:16 KJV

Where does this boldness come from? First, it comes from our citizenship rights. With our redemption, purchased through Jesus' blood, we "are no longer foreigners," or strangers, in God's Kingdom, but we are "fellow citizens with God's people and members of [His] household."[13] Our "citizenship is in heaven."[14] In ancient times, only the citizens of a kingdom had the right to approach the king's throne and speak to him. Now we have been given the right to approach the King of kings. In addition, we have a High Priest (Jesus) in heaven who not only understands us,[15] but also sits "at the right hand of the throne of the Majesty" and intercedes for us.[16]

Boldness comes from having the Holy Spirit in our hearts, too. When we believe in Jesus and accept Him as our Redeemer, the Bible says that the Lord accepts us in return by giving the Holy Spirit to us.[17] The Holy Spirit marks us with a seal[18]—the seal of approval from our King. We are accepted by God!

Boldness is birthed from confidence, and we have confidence because of the promises of Jesus.[19] Before Jesus made a way for us, only the high priest could approach the presence of God in the Holy of Holies, and only once a year at that. However, through the sacrifice of Jesus, we now have confidence to enter God's holy presence at any time.[20]

With the power of the Holy Spirit and the grace of God, we can be confident in our right to boldly approach the presence of God.

Chapter 2
WHAT ARE ADDICTIONS?

According to a booklet released by the National Institute on Drug Abuse, *addiction* is defined as "a chronic, relapsing brain disease that is characterized by compulsive drug seeking and use, despite harmful consequences." [21] Although this definition is specific for drug addiction, it can be extrapolated to all addictions. Basically, an addiction causes someone to compulsively continue pursuing a harmful activity despite its detrimental aftermath.

TYPES OF ADDICTIONS

The word *addiction* most often conjures images of back-alley "druggies" shooting up heroin or some other terrible drug. It is true that the most recognized and prevalent addictions are to drug-related substances. This is not surprising, given the enormous numbers of new drug users we see in this country every year.

According to the 2014 National Survey on Drug Use and Health, the following large numbers of people (ages twelve years and older) had tried drugs for the first time within the previous twelve months:[22]

- Alcohol: 4.7 million new users (12,800 a day)
- Cigarettes: 2.2 million new users (5,900 a day)
- Smokeless tobacco: 1.0 million new users (2,800 a day)
- Marijuana: 2.6 million new users (7,000 a day)
- Pain relievers: 1.4 million new users (3,900 a day)
- Tranquilizers: 1.1 million new users (3,100 a day)
- Hallucinogens: 936,000 new users (2,600 a day)
- Ecstasy: 676,000 new users (1,900 a day)
- Cocaine: 766,000 new users (2,100 a day)
- Methamphetamine: 183,000 new users (500 a day)
- Crack cocaine: 109,000 new users (300 a day)
- Inhalants: 512,000 new users (1,400 a day)
- Heroin: 212,000 new users (600 a day)

We often connect addiction with the misuse of substances like those listed above; however, medical professionals are beginning to include compulsive behaviors that involve sex, video games, and gambling as being addictions, too. (During the writing of this book, gambling was the only *officially* recognized behavioral addiction.)

Sinful pleasures are another type of potential addiction. In fact, they are so dangerous that the Lord lists in Proverbs 6:16–19 the top seven, which have become known as the Seven Deadly Sins. While the most recognized sinful pleasures are extramarital sex and pornography, others are less noticeable but equally addictive. For example, some people are adrenaline junkies who get hooked on performing dangerous activities that tend to increase in risk and intensity in order to produce the same high. Others may get their adrenaline "high" by starting fights and/or causing dissension, and then enjoying the heat of the battle. Some people are addicted to gossip and cannot wait to get the next juicy tidbit.

Food is another sinful pleasure, and overconsumption of it falls into the gluttony category. Although the idea of food addiction is controversial, anyone who struggles with it can attest to the battle to escape it. People can be addicted to eating too much or obsessed with eating too little.

In a study of individuals with various body weights (from underweight to extremely obese), participants were asked about their willingness to make a range of personal sacrifices in exchange for not being obese.[23] Of the participants, 46 percent of them would waive one year of their life rather than be fat, 15 percent would waive ten years, 25 percent would agree to have no children, and 30 percent would rather be divorced than obese. Of the participants who were overweight, 14 percent indicated they would rather be alcoholics than be obese. The sobering statistics from this study are made even more evident by the estimation of thirty-three billion dollars being spent yearly on diet products and weight loss programs.

The science of food addiction is relatively new, but even so, there is evidence that addiction to food is similar to an addiction to drugs in terms of their location in the brain and the types of biochemicals involved. Researchers suggest that the brain mechanisms that drive people to obtain and consume food are the same ones that are hijacked when someone becomes addicted to a drug. Just like with drugs, food addiction involves tolerance, withdrawal, and other similar phenomena.

Basically, as human beings we have a tendency to become addicted to almost anything we enjoy, if we allow ourselves. People can be bound by chocolate, soda, and junk food, just as easily as by cigarettes or alcohol. I believe many people are hooked on cell phones and social media, and if you don't believe me, then try going a few days without it. Even exercise and healthy living can become an obsession.

You might be wondering how in the world exercise could be addictive. Well, my personal obsession with jogging is a shining example. I have been known to jog to the point of physical injury, thus landing me in the emergency room. Like others who love to run, I have even planned my day around jogging, instead of planning my jogging around my day. Although it has been a process, I am learning to use moderation in my passion. I still have friends, though, who continue to run despite feet that require regular cortisone shots and knees that need replacement.

The bottom line is that an addiction is an addiction, and the *only* healthy addiction is being addicted to His presence.

CAUSES OF ADDICTION

Although addictions have been around since almost the beginning of time, it was not until the 1930s that science began seriously studying addictive behavior. Early conclusions from scientists pointed toward flawed morals and lack of willpower as the cause of addictions in people.

Modern science now tells us that both biological and environmental factors affect a person's chances of becoming an addict. Studies have shown that genetic factors account for between 40 and 60 percent of a person's vulnerability to addiction.[24] In addition, children of addicts are eight times more likely to develop addictions themselves.[25] Other risk factors for drug addiction include aggressive behavior in childhood, lack of parental supervision, poor social skills, drug experimentation, availability of drugs at school or work, and community poverty.[26]

Despite all the scientific statistics, no one really knows who will become addicted. The good news is that our genes are not our destiny. God determines our destiny, and the surrendering of our lives to Him is the beginning of our healing process. Lots of people have come from addicted families, but they managed to overcome the curse of the addiction. I am one of those people. Although I have many family members with addictions to alcohol or other substances or behaviors, I was made new and clean from these generational tendencies when I accepted Jesus as my Healer and Restorer. Every day, I continue to renew my mind and declare my victory over the enemy's snare of addiction.

Since the 1930s, scientific discoveries have revolutionized our understanding of the mechanism behind the development of addiction. The cycle of addiction generally starts with innocent intentions to feel good, to perform better, or to satisfy a curiosity. At first, users feel like they can control themselves, but each time they become more tolerant to the effects and soon need more to reach the same level of pleasure.

Science has shown that the dopamine system (which is the body's reward system) is involved with the onset and development of addictions. When certain drugs are consumed, the amount of dopamine that is subsequently released is up to ten times the amount released during activities such as eating or sex.[27] To adjust to this overwhelming surge in dopamine (and other neurotransmitters), the body will turn down the system, much like we would turn down a radio playing too loudly. The body does this by decreasing its production of dopamine and by reducing the number of receptors that can receive dopamine signals. As a result, future signaling via the dopamine system is dulled, and the person's ability to experience pleasure is reduced, thereby necessitating more drug to get the same pleasure as before.

Stress is a major factor in the initiation of addictions. Because people want a "quick fix," they are inclined to turn to things like drugs, food, gambling, or even shopping. When I was a full-time teacher, I remember many other teachers talking about their weight gain over the years as a result of stress eating once they arrived home at the end of each day. Many people choose to self-medicate their problems instead of overcoming them.

Mental disorders such as anxiety, depression, and schizophrenia may precede addictions. In other cases, drug abuse may exacerbate those mental disorders, especially in people who are prone to these vulnerabilities. Some people who suffer from social anxiety use drugs to feel more confident and mask insecurities.

Although the knowledge surrounding addiction grows each day, the medical and scientific community cannot completely explain the *why* of it. I personally believe we focus too much on the physical side of addiction and not enough on the spiritual side. This oversight causes us to miss the root cause of addiction.

Every day, each of us longs to fill the void in our lives that started when Adam and Eve fell into sin, causing all of mankind to be separated from the presence of God. Many people choose to fill this void with worldly pleasures, making a way for addictions to creep in and destroy their lives.

IMPLICATIONS OF ADDICTIONS

The dangers of addictions are real. They can be far-reaching and even result in death. The primary effects of addiction manifest as medical and social consequences in the addict's life; however, the fallout creates a rippling effect that wreaks havoc in the lives of others, as well.

My sister Karen was one of the most beautiful people in the world, both inside and out. At the tender age of fourteen she began to hang out with the wrong crowd and dabbled in drugs. The small things became big and her struggle became real. Over the years, I watched her wrestle with addictions in several areas of her life. Karen is one of the main reasons I am so passionate about sharing the addiction-breaking power of the presence of God.

Addictions will ravage the addict's body and can lead to diseases such as cancer. For example, research has shown that tobacco smoke can cause several cancers. [28] In addition, inhalants are toxic to nerve cells and may destroy the brain and peripheral nerves. Drug users who use syringes are at a very high risk for contracting HIV, hepatitis, and other infectious diseases. Other addicts who struggle with the overconsumption of food and have resulting obesity are prone to heart disease and diabetes.

Addictions can also devastate the addict's relationships, careers, and self-esteem. Adolescents who abuse drugs of any kind do poorly in school and are more prone to drop out. They also place themselves at a higher risk for unplanned pregnancies and crime. Being a teacher, I have witnessed these outcomes firsthand in the lives of my students.

Addictions harm more than just the addict. For example, the negative effects of prenatal drug use are devastating to the unborn. I've seen newborn babies racked with convulsions caused by their mother's crack or meth addictions. Oftentimes, children of drug addicts inherit physical abnormalities, behavioral disorders, and learning disabilities. Another example, secondhand smoke, has been proven to be harmful, and exposure to it increases the risks of heart disease and lung cancer by 25 to 30 percent in people who have never smoked.[29]

Addictions especially hurt family members. Parents who abuse alcohol or drugs bring chaos and stress into the home. The accompanying child abuse and neglect sets up a generational disaster in that family. Children who abuse drugs cause emotional and financial burdens on the rest of the family.

Addictions have negative effects on society, too. The total costs of substance abuse in the United States are estimated to exceed $600 billion annually.[30] This amount includes approximately $193 billion for illicit drugs,[31] $193 billion for tobacco,[32] and $235 billion for alcohol.[33] These costs create a financial strain on the economy, particularly for health care.

Injection drug use contributes to the spread of infectious diseases, and it accounts for about 12 percent of new HIV cases.[34] Any addiction that interferes with judgment or increases the likelihood of risky sexual behavior contributes to the spread of sexually transmitted diseases. The increase and spread of any diseases denigrates the overall health of our society.

The most serious consequence of addiction is the potential for the eternal death of the addict and those friends and family within their influence. By filling the void in their lives with anything other than God, the addict sets up the addiction as an idol. The object of addiction becomes everything to the addict, who lives in constant pursuit of it and forgoes the pursuit of God and the eternal salvation He offers.

OVERCOMING ADDICTIONS

Yes, it is true that God's holy Presence will break addictions; however, sometimes the Lord requires us to put forth effort, too.

Death to Denial
Joyce Meyer once wrote a book on addictions titled *Approval Addiction*, and despite it being one of her favorite books she had written, it was her lowest-selling book to date. She asked her staff to research the disparity. After much investigation, they concluded that people with addictions do not like to admit they have them. In other

words, addicts prefer to live in denial, and nobody wants to believe they are an alcoholic or a drug addict.

I often wonder why it is particularly difficult for Christians to admit to having a problem, especially considering that we are a forgiven people and the Bible says there is no condemnation for those who are in Jesus.[35] One reason, I believe, is that the Church as a whole is perceived as being judgmental, and people fear potential rejection and hurt. Christians feel they cannot be honest, so they go on living in their issues and addictions, all the while perpetuating the image of hypocrisy to the unsaved. As Christians, we need to understand that we are all under grace but the enemy is at work in our lives trying to intimidate and confuse us.

Most of us know that with any problem we want to overcome, we first must admit the problem and claim our responsibility in it. We cannot conquer what we won't confront. We must bring death to our denial.

Treatment
When treating an addiction, it is important that treatment addresses the whole person, including the body, mind, and spirit. Clinicians often use a multifaceted approach to addiction treatment, which may include medication, counseling, support groups, or any combination thereof.

Although it may not seem intuitive, clinicians will often use medication to treat drug addiction. For example, tobacco addictions are frequently treated with nicotine replacement therapies (i.e., a patch, an inhaler, or gum), bupropion, and varenicline. Alcohol and various drug addictions are treated with naltrexone, disulfiram, and acamprosate. Opioid addictions are treated with methadone, buprenorphine, and naltrexone. It is important to note that some of the mentioned prescription drugs have the potential to cause addiction as well as cure it; therefore, the addict must be closely monitored throughout therapy.

Behavioral therapies are used to teach the recovering addict how to replace bad habits with good ones, as well as how to cope with difficult situations. The focus deals with behaviors, thoughts, and feelings that might be causing the underlying problem leading to the addiction.

One of the most important aspects to addiction recovery is having a solid support network. Support groups provide a safe environment for the addict and his or her family to get emotional help and learn about additional helpful resources.

When the addict and family seek to join a support group, it is best to first seek guidance from the family physician or the addiction counselor to help with selection.

A quick Internet search will illustrate the exhaustive list of available groups for every kind of addiction. Following is a very brief list as an example of some various ones.

- *Center for Addiction (www.drug-alcohol-treatment-centers.org)
- *Rehab Angels (www.rehabangels.com/Recovery)
- * Alcoholics Anonymous (www.aa.org), Al-Anon (www.al-anon.org), and Alateen (www.al-anon.alateen.org/for-alateen)
- * Celebrate Recovery (www.celebraterecovery.com)
- * Food Addicts Anonymous (www.foodaddictsanonymous.org)
- * Gamblers Anonymous (www.gamblersanonymous.org)
- * Sexaholics Anonymous (www.sa.org)

Pray and Ask God for Help
God is concerned about every detail of our lives, and He desires for us to come to Him for help. When addictions threaten to overtake you, turn to God first and allow Him to comfort you instead. Pray for strength, guidance, and direction. Don't be afraid to be honest with Him.

When temptations reenter your mind, replace those thoughts with the promises that God has already spoken over you. Meditate on them until the desires pass and peace comes. Here are a few of my favorites.

> John 16:33 NKJV: "These things I have spoken to you, that in Me you may have peace. In the world you

will have tribulation; but be of good cheer, I have overcome the world."

1 Corinthians 15:57 NKJV: But thanks be to God, who gives us the victory through our Lord Jesus Christ.

Romans 8:28 NIV: And we know that in all things God works for the good of those who love him, who have been called according to his purpose.

Philippians 4:13 NKJV: I can do all things through Christ who strengthens me.

Chapter 3
Becoming Addicted to His Presence

Drug addiction starts with an initial taste of pleasure that develops into a strong desire for more. The focus of the addict's life ultimately becomes the pursuit of an elusive high. Addicts will morph into someone unrecognizable as they surrender their lives to the substance and forfeit their self-worth to the enemy, who replaces it with shame and regret.

When we become addicted to His presence, we follow a similar process, that is, we taste of Him, desire more of Him, move our focus to Him, and change our behavior.

TASTE AND SEE THAT THE LORD IS GOOD

After the night my mother and I attended the Spirit-filled revival, she started changing. Something different was happening to her, and I could see it. She starting seeking God like there was no tomorrow. She prayed for what seemed like days on end. I couldn't remember her ever doing stuff like this before, but I continued to question it all.

I remained in a state of fascination with my mom's newfound love interest, until one night when I attended a service at another church. During the exuberant worship, something foreign began to stir in me. I didn't understand what was happening, and to be quite frank, the new sensation induced a bit of fear, and yet, at the same time it felt awesome. It was like something reached down inside of me and woke up my spirit. I felt myself coming alive for the first time in my life. Then, all of a sudden, a warm feeling of love swept over me and I felt an unconditional love like never before. I wanted to bask in it forever and never leave the moment. That night, I encountered the God of love and I was never going to be the same again. I finally understood what had happened to my mother. She had encountered the living God, too, and she wanted more and more of Him, just like I now did.

Not only did my mother and I get a taste of God and like it, but everyone in our family wanted to try it, too. All I know is that those long and tearful prayers of my mother had been answered, because my sisters and I encountered the same loving God she did.

Our first taste of God's presence ignited a hunger in us to want more of Him. I needed His presence. I longed for it. I begin to think about Him more, dream about Him, and talk about Him. A whole new world opened up to me, and today I'm still chasing God over thirty years later. And you know what? I'm still hungry for more.

I challenge you today to taste the Lord's presence and see that it is good!

> *O taste and see that the L*ORD *is good.*
> —Psalm 34:8 KJV

BECOME LOVESICK

Whether you have experienced young love firsthand or vicariously through Hollywood portrayals, you know the excitement and emotional thrills it affords.

When two people are deeply in love, you can almost see their hearts skipping a beat each time they brush up against each other. Their eyes seem to melt into gooey pools when they glance at each other from across the room. Separation from each other becomes their biggest dread because they long to be with each other constantly, and then they count the minutes during the times when they are apart. Sometimes they will drive all night just to share a few moments together. They are unabashedly lovesick for each other, and they don't care who sees it.

People who are lovesick for God will travel hundreds of miles just to get into His presence among other like-minded and lovesick folks. They will do whatever it takes and pay whatever the cost to get to Him. Where did they get this idea? From the Lord, of course. God has been lovesick for us since before the foundation of time. He created us and knew us before we were formed in our mothers' wombs.[36] In fact, He loves us so much that He sent Jesus all the way from heaven to die for our sins. Now, that's a love that surpasses even the greatest distance and cost!

The first time I encountered the presence of God, it was love at first sight. I become lovesick for Him just like the couple I mentioned earlier who were in love. Once you get a taste of His penetrating and endless love, you will, too. You will desire to be with Him all the time. When you wake up, you will find yourself already thinking of Him. You will spend your day fellowshipping and talking with Him, all the while meditating on His will and reading His promises of love recorded in the Bible. That initial taste begets a lovesickness, which in turn creates a desire for more of His presence.

I challenge you today to become lovesick for the Lord!

Jesus replied: "Love the Lord your God with all your heart and with all your soul and with all your mind."
—Matthew 22:37 NIV

Make Him Your Highest Priority

To make God our highest priority means that we purposely value Him above all and we reverence His thoughts and plans above our own.

When two people are in love, they want to learn everything there is to know about each other. They will spend untold hours talking and sharing their past and the dreams of their future. God already knows us inside and out. He even knows how many hairs are on our heads![37] But can we say the same about Him? Have we made it a priority to know Him?

If we just take a moment to reflect on what we know about God based on our surroundings, we can quickly appreciate that there is no end to His coolness. He's the Painter who creates magnificent skies for us, never duplicating the beauty. He's the Musician who sings to us with His wind and the rustling leaves. He watches us as we sleep every night and sends us dreams to prepare us for the coming day. And when we awake, He has fresh new mercies waiting on us so that we never have to live in the past. We haven't seen even a fraction of the creatures He has created. There is no end to His awesomeness. When we are getting to know other people, there comes a time when all the stories have already been told. Not with God, though. There is no possibility of getting bored when eternity isn't long enough to learn everything amazing about Him. The more time we spend with Him, the more we will learn (and want to learn) about Him.

In addition to learning about the character of God, the more time we spend with Him, the more we will ascertain of His master plan and how it applies to our lives. God promises that He has a blueprint for our lives. Have we made it a priority to know it?

> *"For I know the plans I have for you," declares the LORD, "plans to prosper you and not to harm you, plans to give you hope and a future."*
> —Jeremiah 29:11 NIV

The more time we spend with God, the more we believe that He really does have our best interests at heart. This belief leads to trust, and eventually we will begin to value His perfect will over our own self-destructive one. However, just because we may agree with or even like God's plan, that does not mean we have surrendered ourselves to it.

Surrender is not always the easiest thing to do. I am not proud of this, but I admit that surrender is my biggest challenge since becoming a Christian. There's something about our human nature that wants to hang on to things, just in case. Let's be honest here—it's caused by doubt. We struggle to close the door on our backup plans because in our hearts, we doubt that things will go according to the plan. As a result, we tend to "help God out" by tweaking the plan.

This isn't Burger King, folks. We cannot always "have it our way" like their slogan implies. I personally know people who boast about doing things their way, despite the fact that more often than not, they end up with disastrous results. One friend in particular requested the song "My Way" by Frank Sinatra for her funeral. This was a sad request, considering that her life was mostly made up of poverty, sickness, sadness, and anger. Perhaps having it her way was not such a good idea.

Moses was another person who did things his way. As described in the book of Exodus in the Bible, God gave Moses specific instructions to *strike* a rock in order to miraculously release water for the parched people. Moses followed the command and everything worked as planned. However, a while later, Moses found himself in a similar situation, and this time God told him to *speak* to the rock in order to release the water. But instead, Moses struck the rock like before. Moses rejected God's instruction and took matters into his own hands. His disobedience cost him the Promised Land, for he was never permitted to enter and instead was buried in the desert.

Making God our highest priority means that we value Him and His ways above all others and that we place our entire focus on Him.

I challenge you today to make Him your highest priority!

> "But seek first his kingdom and his righteousness, and all these things will be given to you as well."
> —Matthew 6:33 NIV

EMBRACE THE CHANGE

An old bit of folklore suggests that after two people are married for a long while, they begin to start looking and acting alike. The same can be said for our relationship with God. Right from the moment we receive the Holy Spirit, we begin a transformation process to make our character more like His.

> "<u>I will cleanse you</u> from all your impurities and from all your idols. <u>I will give you</u> a new heart and put a new spirit in you; <u>I will remove from you</u> your heart of stone <u>and give you</u> a heart of flesh. And <u>I will put</u> my Spirit in you <u>and move you</u> to follow my decrees and be careful to keep my laws."
> —Ezekiel 36:25–27 NIV, emphasis added

The Bible also says that we are to put on a new self, which was created to be like God in true righteousness and holiness. [38] God Himself says, "Be holy, because I am holy."[39]

God has many attributes other than righteousness and holiness. In Galatians 5:22–23, the Bible gives us a list of the fruits of the Spirit (which are visible characteristics of a changed life that looks more like God): love, joy, peace, patience, kindness, goodness, faithfulness, gentleness, and self-control. When you spend time with God, you will take on these characteristics.

The more that God's presence changes you, the more changes you will want. Slowly your desires for the world will diminish and the desire for God's Kingdom will increase. When my personal life began to change, I lost the desire to hang out with some of my so-called friends, especially those fond of gossiping, backbiting, and partying. I realized that something was happening to me, and I knew I would never be the same. It didn't happen overnight, but with each day, week, and year that passed, my preferences and character changed. I lost many of my desires for sin and gained a new thirst for righteousness.

True change only comes from an encounter with God. Religious doctrine cannot transform anyone. Religion tells people to get their act together and change themselves. Jesus said, "Come to me, all you who are weary and burdened." [40] Psalm 147:3 says that God "heals the brokenhearted and binds up their wounds" (NIV). It's the presence of God that brings real and lasting change.

I challenge you today to embrace the change!

> *Do not conform any longer to the pattern of this world, but be transformed...*
> —Romans 12:2 NIV

RESIST THE ENEMY

The Bible instructs us to "resist the devil, and he will flee."[41] However, before you can resist the enemy, you first need to be able to spot him.

After the fall of mankind into sin, the devil was given dominion over the earth. Since then, he has been constantly making accusations against us before the throne of God. His primary purpose is to keep us separated from God, and he continually works to block our fellowship with Him. He knows that if we ever get into the presence of God, we will be forever changed and thus be lost to his kingdom of darkness.

The best way to identify the enemy is to recognize his voice. It's the one that sounds like guilt, shame, condemnation, worthlessness, etc. He will whisper things like, *Who do you think you are, attempting to approach God? Don't you remember what you did just yesterday?*

Satan is the father of lies. He tries to convince us that we are not good enough to approach God or that our sin is too great. Don't buy in to these lies. If Satan is holding you hostage with past sin, then stop procrastinating and ask God to forgive you. The Bible says that once He forgives our sin, He tosses it into a sea of forgetfulness.⁴² If God can forgive *and* forget our sin, then so should we.

I remember one time when a beautiful young lady wanted to attend a church service with me. I had invited her several times but with no success. When I asked her why she was so hesitant to attend, her answer astonished me. She said she was afraid of God because she had done so many bad things in her life. I was saddened that the deception of God's true love had crept in and kept her from being all God wanted her to be. She had turned to drugs and alcohol because of the deeper longing for a personal relationship with Jesus. After showing her many scriptures on forgiveness and grace, she repented and received Jesus as her Savior. She agreed to attend church and has been a happy Christian ever since.

Another lie that Satan uses is that once people commit to Christ, then they will no longer have any fun. He convinces them that the only fun to be had involves sinful pleasures, which are no longer permissible. Again—very far from the truth. In fact, Christians are supposed to be "filled with an inexpressible and glorious joy."⁴³ The King James Version calls it "joy unspeakable and full of glory."

Satan is also the father of deception, and he uses distractions to keep us from entering into fellowship with God. He fills our day with time-eating tasks and emotions (such as worrying). He uses things like social media, last-minute requests, sickness, arguments, and stress to keep our minds off of God.

I challenge you today to resist and rebuke the enemy from your thoughts and life!

> *Resist the devil, and he will flee from you.*
> —James 4:7 NIV

Chapter 4
Benefits of Being Addicted to His Presence

We all have a longing to be home—not for our earthly house, but a longing to return to companionship with our Creator. When we get into His presence, not only is our longing fulfilled, but we find so much more!

We Find Wholeness and Restoration

The Bible tells a story about how His presence brings wholeness.[44] Jesus was traveling on His way to Jerusalem when He encountered ten men who had leprosy. The men stood at a distance and cried out, "Jesus, Master, have mercy on us!" Jesus replied by telling them to show themselves to the priest (meaning that they were now healed and thus needed the priest to grant them permission to reenter society). The ten men turned from Jesus and headed for the priest. However, when one of the men realized that he had been healed from the disease, he returned and threw himself at Jesus' feet, thanking Him. Jesus responded by making him whole again. In other words, not only was he healed from the disease, but his body no longer bore evidence of ever having had it. Although all of the ten lepers were healed, only one got in His presence and was also made completely whole.

God is in the restoration business. Jesus said that the enemy comes to kill, steal, and destroy, but that He comes so that we can have life, and have it more abundantly.[45] When we get into the presence of God, we can get back what the enemy has taken from us. God has done it for others, and He will do it for you, too. "God does not show favoritism,"[46] "for there is no partiality with God."[47] It does not matter what social class or ethnicity you are, because the Bible says that the Lord is Lord over all who call upon Him.[48] Jesus died for *everyone*, and everyone who believes on Jesus is born of God.[49] Here are some of God's promises of restoration for your life.

> **Health**: He will restore you from your bed of illness.[50] He will restore health to you and heal your wounds.[51]

Time: He will "repay you for the years the locusts have eaten."[52]

Resources: He will "restore your fortunes before your very eyes."[53]

Mind: He will restore your sanity.[54]

Honor: He will restore your honor.[55]

Purity: Though your sins are like scarlet, you will be made white as snow.[56]

Position: He will return your "honor and praise among all the people on earth."[57]

Joy: He will restore the "joy of your salvation."[58]

Soul: He will restore your soul.[59]

Comfort: He will restore comfort to you.[60]

The Lord has an abundance of good things stored up for us,[61] and He is able to bless us abundantly, so that we have what we need when we need it.[62] In fact, He knows what we need before we even ask.[63]

WE GET RELATIONSHIP INSTEAD OF RELIGION

According to the *Merriam-Webster Dictionary*,[64] one of the definitions of the word *religion* is "an organized system of beliefs, ceremonies, and rules used to worship a god or a group of gods."

Religion is *not* what God wants to have with us. *He wants relationship.* Religion has never changed anyone, but an encounter with God changes everyone. Being a Christian should be about seeking God and having an intimate relationship with Him instead of following a bunch of rules.

When two people are in a relationship, they care for each other. God cares about even the smallest things in our lives. I remember one time when I had lost a small object in my house. My friend was visiting and we were in a hurry to attend a meeting, so in a quick moment of prayer, I simply said, "Father God, where is my object?" As I was putting on my raincoat, I stuck my hand into my jacket pocket and found it. I felt the love of my heavenly Father in that very moment. Something that was important to me—even though it was small—became important to Him because He loves me. Religion did not help me find that item—relationship did.

WE GET FREEDOM

The Bible says that people are slaves to "whatever has mastered them,"[65] and therefore, along with addiction comes bondage. However, there is good news because "where the Spirit of the Lord is, there is freedom."[66] The Lord wants "to bind up the brokenhearted [and] to proclaim freedom for the captives."[67]

The bondage of unforgiveness is a huge epidemic in our society. It's a bondage that can even cause us to miss heaven. The Bible says that we are to forgive or we won't be forgiven.[68] If we don't forgive someone, then God doesn't forgive them, either;[69] however, He does forgive them when we ask Him to.[70] Although it can be difficult to forgive others, probably the greatest tragedy takes place when people cannot forgive themselves. The more time we spend in the Lord's presence, the less room in our hearts we have for the chains of unforgiveness and bitterness.

Depression is another shackle the enemy uses to bind up people. Most people feel anxious or upset at times in their lives. If you've been through a divorce, lost a loved one, or experienced any other difficult situation, then you know what I mean. When I use the word *depression*, though, I'm not talking about simply feeling sad or nervous; I'm talking about the type of depression that makes it difficult to carry on a normal life or routine. I deal with this kind of depression on occasion. Sometimes I can be minding my own business, having a good day, and then it seems to hit me out of nowhere. When this happens, I immediately seek the Lord and His presence. In His presence, we can find peace in the storm called depression and we can also find guidance on how to deal with the clinical components of it.

If you are in the presence of the Lord, then freedom is available to you. This includes the freedom of no more shame, guilt, condemnation, or people-pleasing. The world is full of testimonies of how the Lord's presence can break drug and alcohol addiction. Some of these escapes happen even in the midst of intoxication, and the addicts instantly sober up when they experience the God who sets captives free.

We Find Our Purpose

Every person ever created has been designed by God to fulfill a specific purpose on the earth. I never really understood the depth of this until 3 a.m. on the eve of one Thanksgiving holiday. A vision of a favorite old photo kept coming up before my eyes. The photo was of my mother and my sisters dressed up in their white frilly dresses and bonnets. I wasn't visible in the photo because I was still in my mother's growing belly. The image hovered before my eyes, as I heard God's still, small voice saying over and over, "I knew you before you were in your mother's womb." Although my logical mind was still half-asleep, my spirit was wide awake and drinking in the depths of this revelation. My heart was filled with a newfound thankfulness that my heavenly Father knew me before time began and that He knows me still today.

My life is not just a series of unrelated events; instead, it is a collection of both good and bad events that all work together to help me fulfill my purpose on this earth. My one small life among millions of others is important to God—and so is yours. He has great plans for each of us. All of the brokenness we've been through will be used for the good of others, to help them come out of their own pit. We all have a purpose to fulfill on this earth. God knows what that purpose is before we are even born, and it's our job to discover it afterward.

So many people are longing for purpose. They are questioning their existence on earth, whether or not it has any value. One of the biggest mistakes people make is to seek their purpose instead of the One who created them for that purpose. Jesus told us to seek God first, and then everything else would fall into place.[71] The Lord's presence must always be the first priority for us. The more time we spend in His presence, the more clear our purpose will become. In His presence, we find our purpose.

We are to enter the Lord's presence with praise.[72] In order to stay in His presence, we must praise Him all day long. When you wake up, praise Him. Throughout the day, praise Him. While driving down the road, praise Him. When it's nighttime, praise Him. Every time you praise Him, His presence will become even more prominent in your life and your purpose will become even clearer. In addition, because demons run and tremble when they hear the praises of God, they won't stick around to mess up the plans and purposes He has for your life.

Sometimes when we begin to see and walk in God's purpose for our lives, it may become too much to comprehend. When Adam and Eve fell into sin in the Garden of Eden, part of mankind's "brain" fell, as well. Not only did they become aware of their sinful nature, but they lost the revelation knowledge they had had of the supernatural and how it operated. They became limited in their understanding, and now so are we.

God speaks to us in spiritual ways that we cannot decipher with human judgements. Think about it like this. If two people who don't know each other and who speak different languages, which the other does not understand, try to communicate with words, then there will be no understanding. However, the more time these two people spend together getting to know each other, the better they will become at communicating—even if they do not have the same language. The same is true in our relationship with God. The more time we spend in His presence, the more we will understand what He is saying about our purpose and how we can, in fact, accomplish it. We can begin to see things from His point of view.

Some folks have caught a glimpse of their purpose, but they have given up on this dream due to the circumstances of their lives, distractions from the enemy, or unbelief that it could ever happen. Many people are trapped in dry and dead places in life, where it feels like nothing is happening, where all hope is dead, and where there is no refreshing water in sight. Others have built walls around themselves and against God, because life hasn't turned out as they expected. Once these individuals choose to leave their self-induced isolation and enter the presence of God, He will breathe new life into the purpose He has for them.

I once received a letter from a young lady who had been abused nearly all her life and who constantly sought to numb the pain from this abuse with drugs and suicidal ideations. She explained that one day, while she was holding a heroin-loaded syringe just inches from her arm, my *Triumphant Living* program began to play on her radio. As I spoke about the love and power of God, she paused in her intent and began to listen. I continued to speak about never giving up on our God-given dreams, because with God, there is no expiration date or revocation, no matter how far someone has strayed from Him. Tears streamed down her face as the power of the Holy Spirit worked in her heart. She remembered her dreams of wanting to write a book, but she had never felt qualified or she had always been too strung out on drugs or alcohol to accomplish it. That day, after hearing my radio broadcast, the young lady threw her needle and syringe in the garbage, along with all of her other drugs. She chose to fill the void in her life with the presence of God instead of anything else. Today she is drug-free and on the road to wellness and wholeness. But that is not all. At the time of her letter, she held in her hand the first written page of her book. She vows to complete her life story with the help of God, and her goal is to share the testimony of how she was led to freedom by someone speaking life into her at just the right time. This young lady's life is a testimony that in the presence of God, dreams can be resurrected and purpose can be found.

WE EXPERIENCE THE SUPERNATURAL

One of my favorite speakers and authors, Bill Johnson, would always say that the presence of God has been given to us so that we can invade the impossible. I love that!

Mark 9:17–29 tells us of a seemingly impossible situation that was overcome as the result of someone spending time with the Lord. Since childhood, a young boy had been possessed by an evil spirit that threw him to the ground and caused him to have seizures. Sometimes the spirit would throw the boy into fire or water, trying to kill him. It also robbed him of speech and caused him to foam at the mouth and gnash his teeth. Despite their best efforts, Jesus' disciples were unable to expel the evil spirit, and thus, the situation looked grim to the boy's father. The father asked Jesus if He could heal the boy, and Jesus told him that everything was possible for the one who believes. Needless to say, everyone in the presence of Jesus *witnessed* the supernatural when He delivered the boy from the evil spirit. Interestingly, though, only Jesus was able to *perform* the supernatural in this dire situation, because unlike the disciples, He had spent time fasting and praying in His Father's presence beforehand.

If anyone in today's society understands the addiction-breaking power of the presence of God, Todd White does. Todd had been addicted to drugs for twenty-two years, when one night during a drug deal, he was shot at point-blank repeatedly and yet was never hit. Right after his life was supernaturally spared, he received a visitation from God, who spoke to Todd in an audible voice and said, "I took those bullets for you. Are you going to live for Me now?" This radical experience of God's presence changed Todd forever. He went to Teen Challenge to get the help he needed and began to experience one miracle after another. He also began having nightmares that he didn't understand. One day, while he was taking a walk, a homeless man approached him and declared that Todd had demons that needed to leave. He spoke to Todd about his nightmares and the demonic spirits that were oppressing him. Todd didn't really understand it at the time, but he later realized the man was likely an angel from the Lord sent to help him, because the man just disappeared right after talking to Todd. After this encounter, Todd had an accelerated freedom from his addictions. He was completely set free from a twenty-two-year addiction cycle. (See Todd give this testimony at https://www.youtube.com/watch?v=D7TnfHUPnYA.)

The enemy wants to convince us that we are only average people who will always fail at making a positive difference in life. At times he will surround us with other people who want us to fail, too. When we enter into the presence of God, though, these negative influences cannot follow us. In addition, as we reside in His presence and begin to take on the character of God, we transform into people who are anything but average. Instead we are filled with the power and authority we need to accomplish the impossible.

> "With man [addictions may seem to be] impossible, but <u>with God all things are possible</u>."
> —Matthew 19:26 NIV, emphasis added

Chapter 5
EVIDENCE OF BEING ADDICTED TO HIS PRESENCE

When we spend a lot of time in the Lord's presence, it shows.

Look and Sound Different

When we spend a lot of time with God, we start to look and sound more like Him. We become transformed into His image and demonstrate His characteristics (as described in the "Embrace the Change" section earlier in this book).

When Moses spent time in God's presence, his face would radiate and everyone could see it. The same is true with us. When we spend time with the Lord, our faces begin to look different; they may even physically glow with feelings of hope and joy instead of being dulled by despair and defeat. The Bible says that "a happy heart makes the face cheerful,"[73] and that the looks on our faces will testify for us.[74] Therefore, if we have spent time with God, we will have His peace and joy, which will show on our faces and thus testify about His goodness to others.

When the prophet Isaiah was called up to heaven while still living on the earth, the first time he laid eyes upon the Lord, he cried out, "Woe is me! I am a man of unclean lips."[75] What was the Lord's response? He sent an angel to pick up a burning coal from the altar in heaven and place it on Isaiah's mouth to remove his sin and guilt. No doubt—Isaiah never sounded the same afterward. The presence of God will change our "sound," too. For example, the more time we spend with the Lord, the less profanity, foolishness, envious speech, strife-creating words, malicious talk, and evil suspicions will exit our lips. Instead, the Lord will put a new song in our mouths, a hymn of praise to Him.[76] Our mouths will tell of His righteous deeds and His saving acts.[77] As a replacement for "unwholesome talk," our words will speak only "what is helpful for building others up."[78] When we spend time in His presence, our hearts become full of His goodness, which will then flow out of our mouths and become a fountain of life flowing over the lives of others as well as our own.[79]

Before David became the king of Israel, he occupied his young days in the field singing about the Lord's greatness while tending the flocks. His sound was one of praise and worship to the Lord. When the prophet Samuel arrived at David's father's house looking for a king to anoint, David's father, Jesse, presented all of his sons—except for David. In Jesse's and his brothers' eyes, David was just the young boy who tended the sheep; he could not possibly be the next king of Israel. Nobody noticed David very much in his family, but God saw him and ultimately promoted him to be the king. When we spend time in the presence of God, like David did, promotion and favor will come our way.

As we begin to look and sound different after spending time with the Lord, others will see us in a new light, and we will begin to change the way we see ourselves, too. Addictions will destroy many things, but one thing in particular it truly damages is our self-worth. As we spend time in His presence learning who we really are—children of the King—we realize that we were purposely made to accomplish great things while on the earth.

BE A TRUE WORSHIPER

Throughout my life, I have sat in an untold number of church services, each with a very different worship experience. I've seen worship that felt like a funeral service filled with grief and despair, worship that felt like a concert filled with hype, worship that felt like it was taking place in the library quiet zone, and worship that felt like the real deal that is going on in heaven. Despite the general feel of the corporate worship, though, true worshipers can always be easily spotted. They may or may not be the most exuberant ones dancing around, but they are the ones who radiate with the love and adoration they are sending toward heaven.

When you spend time in God's presence and begin to realize that He *really is* the God of all and that He cares about *you*, your heart will be filled with the desire to worship Him, to proclaim thanks and praise for His goodness.

If someone were to walk up to you and hand you both a million dollars and a bottle containing the cure for every disease and illness that plagued your dying body, what would you do? Would you fall down on your knees and thank him over and over? Would you cry? Would you scream with delight while clapping your hands and jumping up and down? What do contestants do on game shows when they win big? When we spend time with God and realize just how much He has given us, how can we not show our thankfulness and become a true worshiper of Him?

True worship connects our hearts to God's. It is more than just singing and clapping. I'm not saying it is wrong to sing, shout, and clap. I am right in there with the best of them when it comes to that. But true worship is filled with love, sincerity, and honor. When you are a true worshiper, you won't need the music to be perfect to "get you started," and you won't need to "feel" His presence to worship Him because you understand that He's always near and that He will never leave you. A true worshiper praises God all day long, every day, instead of only on Sunday mornings, and this worship serves as a testimony to others about the goodness of God.

Have a Heart of Repentance

God's Word says that when we accept Jesus as our Savior, we are made new creations, and like Jesus, we can bury our old dead lives and be resurrected into new ones.[80] When we spend time with God in His Word, we learn about this new life and how to walk in it.

Repentance is the key to embracing this new life. When we spend time in the presence of God, we become more aware of the sin in our lives, and we desire to please God and to rid ourselves of all sin and wrongdoing. Repentance is different from simply being sorry. Feeling sorry means simply feeling bad about something sinful we have done. Repentance is turning away from the sin and never doing it again. The Bible says that "*godly* sorrow brings repentance...and leaves no regret," but "*worldly* sorrow brings death."[81] A heart of repentance is demonstrated by our actions and deeds.[82]

A heart of repentance is dead to sin and alive in Christ. What does this mean? When we spend time in God's presence, we take on His character of holiness and our desires for sin die. The more we repent of our sin, the more we will want to continue to repent.

It is sad but true—some Christians live by the "hyper-grace" doctrine instead of maintaining a repentant heart. This doctrine teaches that all sin (past, present, and future) is forgiven the minute we accept Jesus as our Savior and "confess our sin." This doctrine is so dangerous because many folks are tempted to misuse God's grace as a license to continue sinning. Other people may skirt repentance by continuing to sin but then follow up by asking God for forgiveness, claiming that they are a victim of their sin instead of overcoming it.

Should we go on sinning? By no means! Sometimes we may sincerely repent of a sin and later find ourselves back in it again. The Bible says that each time we have to re-repent about something, it is like crucifying Jesus all over again for our sin.[83] It is just like when we are in love with another person and we don't want to do anything to hurt them—when we are in love with God, we will not want to hurt Him either or let Him down, and we certainly would never want to crucify Jesus over and over for our sins. Instead, we need to crucify our own flesh and its desires.

Forgiving another person is one of the hardest things to force our flesh to do. Nevertheless, a heart of repentance will be demonstrated by acts of forgiveness. Forgiveness is not an option; it is a command.

> *Forgive as the Lord forgave you.*
> —Colossians 3:13 NIV

When we spend time in God's presence and begin to fully acknowledge the amount and depth of forgiveness He has bestowed on us personally, it becomes harder to withhold forgiveness from others. And if the offending person is also a believer, how much more do we need to see them as God sees them—forgiven! When we truly repent of our unforgiveness, we will not only forgive others, but we will also forgive God for the times He was working on our behalf and we saw it as punishment, and we will forgive ourselves for continuing to mess up.

The Bible says that when we repent, God rejoices in the presence of His angels.[84] Can you imagine what happens when you personally repent of some sin? God jumps up from His throne and rejoices, just as if His favorite football team has scored a touchdown!

> *Therefore, since we are surrounded by such a great cloud of witnesses, let us throw off everything that hinders and the sin that so easily entangles, and let us run with perseverance the race marked out for us.*
> —Hebrews 12:1 NIV

WALK DIFFERENTLY

Because our body language can reflect our emotions and mood, the way a person walks is often a reflection of their self-image. Compare the physical walk of a soldier in his dress uniform with that of a homeless veteran in his rags.

A single encounter with God can change the way we walk. Consider Jacob—he spent the night wrestling with God, when finally God touched the socket of his hip.[85] Afterward, Jacob limped physically, and spiritually he was never the same, either.

The more time we spend in the presence of God, the more our spiritual and lifestyle walks will change, too. The first thing that happens is that we get back on track. We begin to walk the ways of the good and keep to the paths of the righteous. We listen for the Lord's voice, telling us, "This is the way; walk in it."[86] Before we take any major steps, we apply prayer and seek Him for our next move. The Lord instructs us to "stand at the crossroads and look; ask for the ancient paths, ask where the good way is, and walk in it."[87] His Word becomes a lamp for our feet and a light on our path.[88]

We will walk with steadiness and surety. Our steps will not be hampered, and when we run, we will not stumble.[89] The Lord says that "when you pass through the waters, I will be with you; and when you pass through the rivers, they will not sweep over you. When you walk through the fire, you will not be burned; the flames will not set you ablaze."[90]

King Saul relentlessly stalked David with the intention of killing him. We all have a similar enemy in our life—the one who won't seem to go away and who tries to steal our footing. When we spend time in the Lord's presence, though, we step into our calling and gain a renewed bounce in our step. It is as if every fiber of our being comes alive.

I have always loved to teach, and I have thoroughly enjoyed watching the kids in my classroom learn and grow. When I began teaching the Bible, though, it was like a light bulb was switched to its brightest setting inside my spirit. I came alive and quickly became addicted to my calling. I couldn't wait for my next opportunity to teach the Word of God. The anointing and presence of God would come upon me, and I loved every minute of what I was doing. It didn't exhaust me the way that merely teaching school did. The bounce in my step was more like a leap.

As we spend time in with God in His Word, we become more mature in our walk. And when we are walking in maturity, we give up selfish desires and will make our requests according to God's will. Jesus said in John 14:13 that He will do whatever we ask in His name. Take a small child, for example. Let's say you read this particular Bible verse to the child. What do you think the child will ask for? Probably all the toys in the mall or maybe a house made up of candy and chocolate. You get my point. The child is not mature enough to ask for things that would benefit a much larger purpose.

The more we experience His presence, the more we will walk with Kingdom-mindedness instead of selfish ambition. I'm not saying that we should not ask for things for ourselves or our families. I'm saying that by staying in His presence, we are more likely to be in line with praying according to His purposes and plans.

Chapter 6
Remaining in His Presence

Adam and Eve took the fruit because they fell for the devil's tricks. Satan used (and he still uses today) many techniques to separate man from God. Getting in God's presence requires effort on our part, but remaining there may require even more.

Use Power and Authority

Power is the ability to do something, but *authority* is the right. Consider a speeding car that is breaking the law. A police officer can hold up a hand and stop it. Why? Because he carries the authority to do so. However, he does not have the power to stop it, because it could run over him. But what if the police officer were also the Hulk? Then he could stop the car with power *and* with authority.

Christians are the spiritual equivalent of a Hulk police officer.

So, where do we get this power and authority? From the Holy Spirit and the name of Jesus. Jesus was endowed with power and authority from His heavenly Father. He gave this power and authority to His twelve disciples, in order to cast out demons and cure diseases.[91] When Jesus died, that power and authority was ultimately made available to everyone who calls upon His name and claims Him as Savior. He has instructed us to use His name when we ask the Father for our requests.[92] His "name" is more than the word *Jesus*. For example, in early history, kings used to give the leaders below them a signet ring that had the king's name or crest engraved on it. The leader would then use that ring to stamp or seal agreements (much like providing the king's signature on a contract). If someone had the king's ring, it meant that he had the power and authority to do kingdom business *in the name of the king*. The Bible says that we are sealed with the Holy Spirit,[93] which is spiritually equal to being a ring bearer for Him. We can do Kingdom business in His name.

We have both power and authority over the enemy in our lives, but it is up to us to enforce it. Using these tools is crucial for a productive Christian walk. If we don't understand how to use them, we will not get very far in resisting the enemy. Following are three stories about people who are learning to use their power and authority. (*Note: The names of these people may have been changed.)

My Story
Depression was no stranger to me through some of my teen years and early twenties. It would come and go in waves, and it made me feel like a yo-yo. I came to accept depression as my lot in life, and I had convinced myself to just tolerate it the best I could.

I can honestly say that revelation didn't come overnight, but as I dug in to the Word of God and spent time in His presence, I began renewing my mind with His promises. I soon realized that I had been believing the enemy's lies about myself and this curse called depression. The Bible says that when we hold to Jesus' teachings, "then you will know the truth, and the truth will set you free."[94] During the time I spent reading the Word, I learned the truth—that I have power and authority over depression and the lies of the enemy and that I can walk in freedom. From then on, each time I would feel depressed or would lack joy, I would simply use my power and authority over the darkness, and the darkness would flee. I would rebuke the lies with the name of Jesus and replace them with the promises of God. Now, when the darkness tries to come back, I am fully equipped with the tools I need to overcome it.

Ann's Story
Ann was a beautiful young lady who had many wonderful gifts and talents. By all natural means, it looked like she was the happiest person alive. However, one day she confided in me that she was battling life-threatening depression and that she would contemplate suicide many times a day. I instantly leapt into action and explained that the enemy is the author of confusion, depression, and every other evil work. I went on to explain the basic concept of power and authority and asked her to believe it as we prayed together for her freedom. She agreed to believe the best she knew how with the knowledge I had quickly given to her. I took her hands in mine and prayed a simple prayer of faith that went something like this: "Father, in the name of Jesus, I command all oppression, depression, and thoughts of death to leave this girl right now. We use our God-given power and authority over this evil spirit." Immediately, Ann declared that she had a wonderful sensation of joy come over her. I could visibly see the change in her countenance. She said it felt like a dark cloud had lifted, and she could suddenly see what her problems had been. She continues to use the tools of power and authority to walk in freedom.

Betty's Story
Betty had finished her shopping and was loading her infant daughter into her car seat when a thief approached her

from behind. She said a supernatural boldness came over her as she recalled reading in the Bible about the name of Jesus. She said she stood straight up, looked the thief square in the eye, and repeatedly yelled, "In the name of Jesus Christ of Nazareth, I command you to leave me now." (Now, picture in your mind this little lady, who is all of five feet tall, shouting commands to a big ol' robber!)

Needless to say, the enemy fled, and she got into her car with her baby and her purse and drove off with no harm.

Although she should have been afraid at the time, Betty deeply understood her rights as a believer and she was able to resist the enemy with power and authority. She went on to say that the Holy Spirt rose up in her, and she felt as bold as a lion, just like the Bible says:

> *The wicked man flees though no one pursues, but the righteous are as bold as a lion.*
> —Proverbs 28:1 NIV

CONTINUAL RENEWING

To remain in the Lord's presence, we must remain free from the things that would separate us from it. The Bible tells us not to let ourselves be burdened again by a yoke of slavery.[95] How do we remain free? By a continual renewing of our minds, our spirits, and our faith.

Romans 12:2 tells us that we are "transformed by the renewing of our mind." To renew our mind, the first thing that we need to do is to "take captive every thought" that does not line up with God's Word and "make it obedient" to Christ.[96] Then we need to replace all of our negative thoughts with God's thoughts. Philippians 4:8 instructs us to think about whatever is true, noble, right, pure, lovely, and admirable. We also need to renew our self-identity in our minds by constantly reminding ourselves of who we are in Christ. We are children of the King. We are redeemed. We are new creatures. Our past, sinful life is dead. We are no longer under the power of the enemy, and we can resist him. We have power and authority through the name of Jesus and the Holy Spirit. We are recipients of all of God's blessings and provision.

Jesus taught about the importance of keeping our spirits renewed and clean. What He says is very sobering:

> "When an evil spirit comes out of a man, it goes through arid places seeking rest and does not find it. Then it says, 'I will return to the house I left.' When it arrives, it finds the house unoccupied, swept clean and put in order. Then it goes and takes with it seven other spirits more wicked than itself, and they go in and live there. And the final condition of that man is worse than the first."
> —Matthew 12:43–45 NIV

When we expel the spirit of addiction from our lives, we need to immediately fill the void—not with other addictions, though, but with the Holy Spirit. Psalm 51:10 says, "Create in me a clean heart, O God; and renew a right spirit within me" (KJV). We must keep our lives occupied with His Spirit living in us. We also must keep ourselves clean, and the way to do this is with repentance.

"Faith is the substance of things hoped for, the evidence of things not seen." [97] We need to renew our faith continually because it is so powerful that even just a little bit can do amazing things. Jesus said that if we "have faith as small as a mustard seed," then we could tell mountains to move and they would obey.[98]

The best way to renew our faith is to remind ourselves of all the things that God has done for us. Keeping a gratitude journal of all the blessings and miracles that God has done in our lives will allow us to go back during the trying times and read about God's grace and mercy, thereby increasing our faith to persevere. Sharing our personal testimony with others will not only increase our faith but theirs, as well.

We can also renew our faith by reading about the ways God works in the lives of other people. Hebrews 11 in the Bible is a tremendous faith builder, as it summarizes how other people were able to keep the faith. Because we know that God is a fair God, when we see Him doing things for His other children, we can know and be encouraged that He will do the same for us.

Probably the greatest way I increase my faith is to seek and recognize the supernatural workings of God. When I feel my faith meter shifting to "low," I start looking for Christian, Bible-based meetings and conferences that focus on healings, miracles, and the manifestation of God. I can't imagine anyone attending these conferences—seeing paralyzed people walk and blind people see—and then walking out without having an increase in their faith. When I witness these things, it makes me want to jump up and down and declare the goodness of God over my own situation!

The Bible says that we are to renew ourselves "*day by day.*"[99] However, I will tell you that there are times in my life when it has to be *minute by minute*. Sometimes I even have to reach out to a trusted friend to help strengthen me, as is described in Acts 14:22.

STAY COMMITTED

To many people, *commitment* is a dirty word. The concept of commitment conjures up ideas of giving up things we like, being obligated to do things we don't want to do, or feeling unjustified when others do not commit at the same level as we do. There is just something about human beings that doesn't like commitment, and no doubt, the origins of our feeling this way came from lies the enemy has whispered (or even yelled) in our ears.

Anyone who has entered into a mutual and trusting commitment with another person knows how it can be very rewarding and comforting. All relationships become better and deeper when a commitment is mutually acknowledged.

God has already acknowledged His commitment to us, actually, over and over again. The Lord has promised, "I will be with you; I will never leave you, nor forsake you."[100] If our relationship with the Lord is to be what it's supposed to be, then we need to commit to Him in return. First Peter 4:19 says that we should commit ourselves to our faithful Creator and continue to do good.

What does it mean to be committed to the Lord? Just like with our other relationships in life, it means that we should be exclusive. The First Commandment tells us to have no other gods before Him, and the Second Commandment says to not make idols. Taken together, these commandments instruct us not to be adulterous with God. We should not value, prefer, or place any other person or thing over Him. What does this look like in real life? It can happen when someone chooses God over television, food, shopping, or other pleasures or addictions.

A commitment means that we are dedicated—that we put energy and work into our relationship. It requires action on our part to be consistent and deliberate. It means that we will keep our word, just like He keeps His.

Our commitment to God has to be all or nothing. We must be all in. The Lord despises middle-of-the-roaders and people who are neither hot nor cold. He says He will vomit the lukewarm ones from His mouth. [101] A true commitment means that even if life gets tough—and it will—we are in for the long haul. In marriage ceremonies, we make a vow that we will remain committed "till death do us part." How much more serious should we take our commitment with the Lord?

STAY FOCUSED

Whatever you focus on is what you will think about. It takes only a few moments for me to chat with someone and discern where their focus is.

The world is full of politics and crime, and the news reporters do a good job at finding stories that excite the ears of their listeners. However, when the focus of our lives becomes all about the immediate situations around us, we start worrying and living in dread instead of fixing our attention on the things of God.

Today's world is also full of "selfies." Sad but true—we have become a narcissistic society. If Lucifer had opened a social media account in heaven when he was there, I wonder what his page would have looked like. No doubt it would have been filled with tons of photos of himself and posts about how great he was. I also wonder if his page would have looked any different from the ones we see in our society today. And we all know what happened when Lucifer took his focus off of the Lord and put it on himself—he had to change the name on his social media page from "Lucifer" to "Satan" and his address from "heaven" to "earth."

Anytime we put God out of our sight and focus on something else (whether it be ourselves, our families, our jobs, the news, etc.), it becomes an idol in our lives. Here are some points you can use every day to help you stay focused on the Lord and His ways.

1. I am forgiven and protected by the Lord. I therefore release all those who have hurt me.
2. I have not missed the Lord's best for my life, so I eagerly await the fulfillment of His promises.
3. My past will not define me, so I release all shame and guilt to the Lord.
4. The Lord will not reject me.
5. The Lord loves me for who I am, and I look for His love daily.

6. The Lord will lead me into right choices and give me strength and direction for my life.

7. The Lord will lead me to people whom I enjoy and they will enjoy me.

8. Nothing will ever separate me from the love of the Lord, and His grace and mercy are always available to me.

9. I will make good choices with the help of the Lord.

10. I can hear the Lord's voice because He desires to fellowship with me.

Don't Look Back

To stay in the presence of God, we cannot continue to run back to worldly ways when things get hard. One of the greatest trials we will ever face is the temptation of looking back. When Lot and his family were escaping the destruction of Sodom and Gomorrah, they were instructed not to look back. Lot's wife gave in to the temptation, and it cost her dearly. When she looked back, she became a pillar of salt.[102]

There are many warnings in the Bible about looking back. One that stands out is a scripture that God spoke to me many years ago when I was in a painful relationship that was very toxic to both my emotional and my spiritual health. We eventually broke up, and through much brokenhearted prayer, I began to experience healing. Just when I thought I was moving on with my life, however, this boyfriend resurfaced and sought reconciliation. Despite the temptation to date him again, I heard the Lord clearly say that any relationship I had with this young man would be detrimental to my life. He pointed me to Proverbs 26:11: "As a dog returns to its vomit, so a fool repeats his folly."[103] Had I chosen to go back, I would have been the fool and I would have had to pay the price again.

The Israelites constantly struggled with the temptation of looking back. They wanted to return to Egypt every time they turned around. Even though they had come out of terrible bondage in Egypt, when things got tough in the desert, their answer was to return to it rather than face the unknown. Isn't it funny how a previous bad situation all of a sudden cannot seem as bad as our current one, even though it really is? (Another trick of the enemy!)

We cannot continue to live like the Israelites, always looking back. Instead, we should take the way of Elisha. When Elisha was called to serve in the Kingdom, he slaughtered his yoke of oxen and burned them with his plowing equipment, and he gave the cooked meat to the people before setting out on his new journey.[104] Elisha symbolically burned his past life so he could never return to it. There was no going or looking back.

Chapter 7
YOU CAN AND YOU WILL OVERCOME

When we reflect back on the Garden of Eden, we know that God intended for mankind to live in perfect peace with Him. However, that fellowship was broken when Adam and Eve sinned in the Garden of Eden. Since then, mankind has longed to reconnect with His presence. There is nothing on this planet that will ever satisfy us or be an adequate substitute for the presence of God in our lives—not drugs, not earthly relationships, not entertainment, nothing.

Remember the Disney movie *Sleeping Beauty*? Princess Aurora bit into an apple and fell into a deep sleep. Like the princess, Adam and Eve bit into an apple and now mankind has fallen into a deep spiritual sleep and we do not even realize it. Many people live and die on this earth and never wake up from this spiritual death. They have never allowed the Prince of Peace, Jesus Christ, to awaken their spirits with His kiss. I know this seems like a childish analogy of how one encounter with God can be so life-changing, but my point is very clear: One intimate moment with God will awaken every fiber of your being and your spirit will become alive once again. It's time to wake up!

Until we understand that the only true satisfaction in life can be found in fellowship with our Creator, Father God, we will always be looking for alternatives to sedate that empty feeling in our lives. This book was written to teach you the importance of the Lord's presence, how to find it, and how to stay there.

Stop the madness of destructive addictions and become addicted to His presence instead. This is what we were born to do. Seek the face of God and allow His presence to fulfill that longing in your soul.

Would you like to reconnect with your Creator? Maybe after reading this book, you are thinking that this is exactly what you've been looking for. If so, pray this prayer out loud.

> Dear Lord Jesus, I know I am a sinner, and I ask for Your forgiveness. I believe You died for my sins and rose from the dead. I trust and follow You as my Lord and Savior. Guide my

life and help me do Your will. I ask that You give me the strength to overcome all addictions and that I would have total balance in my life. Please help me to let go of people who drag me down and to recognize those who really love me and have my best interests at heart. Please help me to know that I can have a happy and addiction-free life that is full of hope. Lord, I seek You and Your presence above everything else.

Did you pray this prayer? If so, please contact us at www.bethstewartministries.com and let us know. We will help you with the next step. Find a good Bible-based church and read your Bible every day. Blessings to you!

.

ABOUT THE AUTHOR

Beth Stewart realized the call on her life when she made a commitment for Christ at the age of seventeen. Her passion is to set the captives free through the truth of Jesus Christ and God's Word.

Beth is the founder of *Triumphant Living* radio ministry and the CEO of Beth Stewart Ministries, which reaches over thirty nations. A Bible teacher, author, public speaker, and radio talk host, Beth also holds a BA in education, an MA in education, and a BS in theology. She speaks to many church groups, conferences, businesses, and organizations in the effort to bring hope and encouragement to help facilitate the fulfillment of destiny and God-given dreams within people.

Dreams NEVER Expire
by Beth Stewart

2015 Readers Favorite Bronze Award

Dreams NEVER Expire uses real-life stories to prove that dreams can be fulfilled no matter the circumstances. If you're looking for a sign to keep on trying, then you've found it here.

ABOUT BETH STEWART MINISTRIES

Beth Stewart Ministries was birthed with a passion to reach a lost and dying world. Our primary goal is to win the lost to Jesus Christ to ensure their salvation. Our mission is to reach around the world to bring the good news of Jesus Christ to as many souls as possible. We are doing this through speaking, books, street ministry, and radio broadcasts.

BSM

BethStewartMinistries.com

Beth Stewart Ministries is a 501(c)(3) nonprofit organization. All donations are tax-deductible. You can donate directly via PayPal at info@BethStewartMinistries.com or mail your donation to Beth Stewart Ministries, 525 West 5th Street, Suite 334, Covington, KY 41011. You can also donate via various other ways. Please see the website for a list.

ACKNOWLEDGMENTS

I would like to acknowledge my sister Karen Sue whom I adored and admired so much for her courage.

I would also like to thank the following people:

W.C. Stewart

Alex and Austin Stewart

Lawrence Bishop II

Dr. Mike Kalfas

Pastor James Turner

Heather May

Jennifer Minigh

REVIEW REQUEST

I hope you have gained some helpful knowledge from *Addicted to His Presence.*

Now that you've read this book, if you enjoyed it, then please let other readers know. Let's share the knowledge, helping other people break the addictions in their lives and find the only true thing that satisfies—the Lord's Presence.

SCRIPTURES AND REFERENCE

1 Matthew 10:8 NIV
2 Romans 6:23 NIV
3 Act V Scene I, *Macbeth*, Shakespeare
4 Psalm 139:23 NIV
5 Matthew 11:6 NKJV
6 "Repent." 2015. In Merriam-Webster.com. Retrieved October 20, 2015, from http://www.merriam-webster.com/dictionary/repent.
7 Hebrews 12:15 NIV
8 Matthew 5:23–24 NIV
9 Ephesians 1:6 NIV
10 Romans 5:2 NIV
11 Romans 3:24 and Ephesians 2:8–9 NIV
12 2 Corinthians 12:9 NIV
13 Ephesians 2:19 NIV
14 Philippians 3:20 NIV
15 Hebrews 4:15 NIV
16 Hebrews 8:1 and Hebrews 7:25 NIV
17 Acts 15:8 NIV
18 Ephesians 1:13 NIV
19 2 Corinthians 3:4 NIV
20 Hebrews 10:19 and Ephesians 3:12 NIV
21 "Drug Abuse and Addiction." Drug Abuse and Addiction. July 1, 2004. Accessed December 2, 2015. https://www.drugabuse.gov/publications/drugs-brains-behavior-science-addiction/drug-abuse-addiction.
22 Rachel Lipari, Larry Kroutil, and Michael Pemberton. "Risk and Protective Factors and Initiation of Substance Use: Results from the 2014 National Survey on Drug Use and Health." NSDUH Data Review: Risk and Protective Factors and Initiation of Substance Use: Results from the 2014 National Survey on Drug Use and Health. October 1, 2015. Accessed December 2, 2015. http://www.samhsa.gov/data/sites/default/files/NSDUH-DR-FRR4-2014 (1)/NSDUH-DR-FRR4-2014.htm.
23 M.B. Schwartz, L.R. Vartanian, B.A. Nosek, K.D. Brownell. The influence of one's own body weight on implicit and explicit anti-fat bias. Obesity (Silver Spring). 2006 Mar;14(3):440–7.
24 "Drug Abuse and Addiction." Drug Abuse and Addiction. July 1, 2004. Accessed December 2, 2015. https://www.drugabuse.gov/publications/drugs-brains-behavior-science-addiction/drug-abuse-addiction.
25 Steven M. Melemis, *I Want to Change My Life: How to Overcome Anxiety, Depression, & Addiction.* Revised ed. Toronto: Modern Therapies, 2010.

26 "Drug Abuse and Addiction." Drug Abuse and Addiction. July 1, 2004. Accessed December 2, 2015.
https://www.drugabuse.gov/publications/drugs-brains-behavior-science-addiction/drug-abuse-addiction.

27 G. Di Chiara, A. Imperato, Drugs abused by humans preferentially increase synaptic dopamine concentrations in the mesolimbic system of freely moving rats. Proc Natl Acad Sci 85:5274-5278, 1988.

28 U.S. Department of Health and Human Services. The health consequences of smoking: a report of the Surgeon General. Atlanta, Georgia. U.S. Department of Health and Human Services, Centers for Disease Control and Prevention, National Center for Chronic Disease Prevention and Health Promotion, Office on Smoking and Health; Washington, DC, 2004.

29 Office of the Surgeon General. "The Health Consequences of Involuntary Exposure to Tobacco Smoke." 2007. Accessed December 2, 2015.
http://www.surgeongeneral.gov/library/reports/secondhandsmoke/fullreport.pdf.

30 National Institute on Drug Abuse; National Institutes of Health; U.S. Department of Health and Human Services. "Understanding Drug Abuse and Addiction." DrugFacts. November 2012. Accessed March 01, 2016.
https://www.drugabuse.gov/publications/drugfacts/understanding-drug-abuse-addiction.

31 National Drug Intelligence Center (2011). The Economic Impact of Illicit Drug Use on American Society. Washington D.C.: United States Department of Justice. Available at:
http://www.justice.gov/archive/ndic/pubs44/44731/44731p.pdf.

32 Centers for Disease Control and Prevention. Smoking-Attributable Mortality, Years of Potential Life Lost, and Productivity Losses—United States, 2000–2004. Morbidity and Mortality Weekly Report. Available at: http://www.cdc.gov/mmwr/preview/mmwrhtml/mm5745a3.htm.

33 J. Rehm, C. Mathers, S. Popova, M. Thavorncharoensap, Y. Teerawattananon, J. Patra, Global burden of disease and injury and economic cost attributable to alcohol use and alcohol-use disorders. Lancet, 373(9682):2223–2233, 2009.

34 Centers for Disease Control and Prevention. HIV/AIDS Statistics Overview. See http://www.cdc.gov/hiv/statistics/index.html.

35 Romans 8:1 NIV
36 Jeremiah 1:5 NIV
37 Matthew 10:30 NIV
38 Ephesians 4:24 NIV
39 Leviticus 11:44 NIV
40 Matthew 11:28 NIV
41 James 4:7 NIV
42 Micah 7:19
43 1 Peter 1:8 NIV
44 Luke 17:11–19 NKJV

45 John 10:10 NKJV
46 Acts 10:34 NIV
47 Romans 2:11 NKJV
48 Romans 10:12 NIV
49 1 John 5:1 NIV
50 Psalm 41:3 NIV
51 Jeremiah 30:17 NIV
52 Joel 2:25 NIV
53 Zephaniah 3:20 NIV
54 Daniel 4:36 NIV
55 Daniel 4:36 NIV
56 Isaiah 1:18 NIV
57 Zephaniah 3:20 NIV
58 Psalm 51:12 NIV
59 Psalm 23:3 NIV
60 Isaiah 57:18 NIV
61 Psalm 31:19 NIV
62 2 Corinthians 9:8 NIV
63 Matthew 6:8 NIV
64 "Religion." 2015. In Merriam-Webster.com. Retrieved October 20, 2015, from http://www.merriam-webster.com/dictionary/religion.
65 2 Peter 2:19 NIV
66 2 Corinthians 3:17 NIV
67 Isaiah 61:1 NIV
68 Matthew 6:15 and Luke 6:37 NIV
69 John 20:23 NIV
70 Numbers 14:20 NIV
71 Matthew 6:33 NIV
72 Psalm 100:4 NIV
73 Proverbs 15:13 NIV
74 Isaiah 3:9 NIV
75 Isaiah 6:5 NIV
76 Psalm 40:3 NIV
77 Psalm 71:15 NIV
78 Ephesians 4:29 NIV
79 Matthew 12:34, 15:18, and Proverbs 10:11 NIV
80 2 Corinthians 5:17 and Romans 6:4 NIV
81 2 Corinthians 7:10 NIV
82 Acts 26:20 NIV
83 Hebrews 6:6 NIV
84 Luke 15:10 NIV
85 Genesis 32:24–31 NIV
86 Isaiah 30:21 NIV
87 Jeremiah 6:16 NIV
88 Psalm 119:105 NIV
89 Proverbs 4:12 NIV
90 Isaiah 43:2 NIV

[91] Luke 9:1 NIV
[92] John 15:16 NIV
[93] Ephesians 4:30 NIV
[94] John 8:32 NIV
[95] Galatians 5:1 NIV
[96] 2 Corinthians 10:5 NIV
[97] Hebrews 11:1 KJV
[98] Matthew 17:20 NIV
[99] 2 Corinthians 4:16 NIV
[100] Joshua 1:5 NIV
[101] Revelation 3:16 NIV
[102] Genesis 19:26 NIV
[103] Proverbs 26:11 NIV
[104] 1 Kings 19 21 NIV